Working with Words
in Business and Legal Writing

Working with Words in Business and Legal Writing

Lynne Agress, Ph.D.

BASIC
B
BOOKS
A Member of the Perseus Books Group
New York

Copyright © 2002 by Lynne Agress
Previously published by Perseus Publishing
Published by Basic Books, a Member of the Perseus Books Group

Cataloging-in-Publication Data is available from the Library of Congress
ISBN-10 0–7382–0562–1
ISBN-13 978–0–7382–0562–5

Text design by *Trish Wilkinson*
Set in 10.5-point Stone Serif by the Perseus Books Group

First printing, April 2002

Contents

Contents

Preface

Writing is not merely putting words on a page. It is using words that make sense, that express an idea in the clearest possible way.

Acknowledgments

I thank the many BWB workshop participants for the examples used in this book. Proper names have been changed or omitted. Parts of the text have previously appeared in articles in *Legal Times* and the *Baltimore Business Journal*.

Credits

Working
with Words
in Business
and Legal
Writing

PART ONE

Words on Writing

Introduction

Despite the current expansion in the use of communication technology, written and verbal literacy is in dramatic decline. Ironically, as our communications proliferate via computer networks, faxes, e-mail and the Internet, we are becoming less and less literate. Our educational system is a convenient culprit. Not all, but many of our schools are woefully underfunded, poorly staffed, and forced to spend more time on policing and less on educating.

Outside of English classes, schools give little attention to grammar, and fewer English teachers require their pupils to diagram sentences. Moreover, many schools no longer require the study of foreign languages (not even Latin, although it is the foundation of English grammar), and some schools would rather teach students to push buttons on computers and calculators than teach them the principles of reason and logic.

As a result, many professional and businesspeople cannot communicate well. Every day—often without knowing it—lawyers, engineers, marketing managers and others lose deals and/or major clients because of poor writing skills. Either the reader misunderstands what the writer has written, or the reader is offended by the tone of a letter or report, by bad grammar, by wordiness and redundancy, by jargon or by other mistakes in communication.

But good writing need not be a dying art. The following chapters are about common mistakes in professional and business correspondence and how to correct them. You can learn to edit your own writing—as well as that of your co-workers and employees—to improve communication with clients, with friends and even with family.

Let's begin with a quiz to test your literacy quotient.

1

How Literate Are You?
A Grammar/Usage Quiz

When you're trying to close that special deal, to impress a new client or hang on to an old one, your English can make all the difference. But you might not write or speak as well as you think you do. Flawed language is more common today than you may realize. Even journalists, newscasters, politicians and talk-show hosts use words, phrases and sentences that are redundant, awkward and just plain wrong.

To test your language skills, choose the statement below that best completes the scenario described. Then turn to page 11 to find your overall literacy rating.

QUESTIONS

1. You've just been asked to give a major presentation to a visiting client from XYZ Industries whose business is much sought after. You stand up and say:

   a. "Today XYZ Industries is making a major contribution."
   b. "At this point in time XYZ Industries is making a major contribution."
   c. "In today's society XYZ Industries is making a major contribution."

2. You've just found out that Charlie, your former boss who always blocked your promotions, is in town. You say to your husband:

   a. "I could care less."
   b. "I couldn't care less."

3. A co-worker says he knows where to get, cheaply, a slightly used Mercedes, a compact stereo system and ski equipment. But somehow he never gives you the names of the dealers, nor does he offer to take you shopping with him. You tell a friend:

   a. "The guy is all talking and no action."

    b. "The guy is all talk and no action."

    c. "The guy just talked, but he doesn't do any-
thing."

4. Alice, the new broker, has just appropriated one of your good accounts. You tell a friend:

    a. "Alice has behaved contemptibly."

    b. "Alice has behaved contemptuously."

5. You and your business partner are trying without success to contact a client. Finally you write a note saying:

    a. "Please phone Thompson or myself."

    b. "Please phone Thompson or me."

6. It's been one of those weeks. You broke your wrist playing racquetball; your Master Card is over the limit; and this morning your car broke down on the Beltway. Reacting, you say:

    a. "I wish I were on a beach in Hawaii."

    b. "I wish I was on a beach in Hawaii."

7. You've been trying, without success, to get Mike O'Malley to merge his small robotics firm with yours. You call your attorney and say:

"And remember—no more subjunctives where the correct mood is indicative."

a. "Tom, you've got to advise me on this matter."
b. "Tom, you've got to advice me on this matter."
c. "Tom, you've got to council me on this matter."
d. "Tom, you've got to counsel me on this matter."

8. You and your wife are planning a formal dinner to which you've invited the president of your company and her husband plus several other company executives and their spouses. You tell a friend that you will be serving:

   a. "gourmet food."
   b. "food delicacies."
   c. "fine food."

9. You're describing to your boss the football game in which the Ravens stomped the Patriots. Except for a touchdown in the first quarter, the Patriots had:

   a. "fewer points during the entire game."
   b. "less points during the entire game."

10. You've just emerged from a tedious staff meeting, but it was worth it; you finally got your point across. Elated, you tell your secretary:

    a. "That was a really good meeting."
    b. "That was a real good meeting."

11. The head of Human Resources tells you that she has heard about an excellent new health benefits program. You ask her:

    a. "Is this different than the plan we already have?"
    b. "Is this different from the plan we already have?"

12. After attending a taping of the *Oprah Winfrey Show,* you tell your co-workers:

    a. "The show was taped before a live audience."
    b. "The show was taped before a studio audience."

Bonus Question

13. The head of your department was recently named Executive Vice President. You're thrilled when his wife calls to invite you and your husband to a dinner party. Since the man and his wife live nearly an hour away, you thank her and add:

    a. "Hopefully, we'll arrive early."
    b. "We will try to arrive early."

ANSWERS

1. *a.* (b) and (c) are unnecessarily wordy. (b) is fast becoming a cliché, and (c) sounds absurd. What was yesterday's society—the Victorian Age, the Anglo-Saxons, Neanderthal Man?

2. *b.* To express indifference, you must choose (b). Logically speaking, if you could care less, as in (a), you actually care a lot. (Maybe you do.)

3. *b.* Only (b) exemplifies correct parallel structure. Words go with similar words, phrases with similar phrases, clauses with similar clauses. (a) uses two different noun forms. In (c), the first verb, *talked,* is past tense. The second, *doesn't do,* is present; furthermore, the verb *do* has a helping verb, *doesn't,* whereas the verb *talked* does not.

4. *a.* If you said (a), you're safe, because *contemptibly* means "deserving of contempt"—which Alice may be, having stolen your client. But if you said (b), which means Alice showed contempt for the client, you're merely a wishful thinker.

5. *b.* Trying to sound formal can backfire. If you eliminate *Thompson* from the sentence, you can see that *me* is the object of the verb *phone.*

6. *a*. You're not in Hawaii, but unfortunately, still at home. *Were* is correctly used with both singular and plural subjects to signal the unreality of the stated fact. This form of the verb *to be* is called the *subjunctive mood*.

7. *a* and *d*. *Advise* and *counsel* are verbs meaning "to help." *Advice* and *council* are nouns. Advice is information you get from others; a council is an assembly, an official body of lawmakers. If Tom advises/counsels you well, then you can act on his advice.

8. *c*. A gourmet, strictly speaking, is a *person* who enjoys fine food. Both food and delicacies are nouns, and a noun cannot modify a noun; only an adjective can.

9. *a*. *Fewer* denotes number; *less* denotes amount or degree. If you answered (b), you might have made fewer points with your boss or left a less positive impression than you imagined.

10. *a*. *Really* is an adverb, and therefore it can modify the adjective *good*. *Real* is an adjective, and adjectives can modify only nouns, not other adjectives. If you answered (b), do you mean that all the other meetings you have attended were unreal?

11. *b.* The preferred preposition after *different* is *from.*

12. *b.* If you said (a), you made the same mistake that many TV announcers have made. The wording in sentence (a) is redundant because all audiences are "live"—unless a few ghosts slip in.

13. *b.* If you said (a), you meant you're full of hope but you still may not arrive on time; so don't expect your hosts to wait.

Give yourself 10 points for each correct answer. If you scored between 100 and 130, you're literate and should have no problems communicating both professionally and socially. But if you scored less than 100, you'd better bone up. Take a course or buy a grammar text and start studying.

2

Cutting Down on Words

In business and the professions, one is always writing for a reader. And most readers are busy people who don't like to waste time reading three pages that easily could have been condensed to less than one.

In writing, more is not better. Yet some writers seem stuck in term-paper mode. In high school, piles of prose, often copied verbatim from the *World Book* or *Britannica* and topped with an attractive cover, might have been the surest way to an A. In the business world, however, wordiness in a memo, letter or report is a turnoff. Although today's executives may be beguiled by a lively cover, they have little time to read what's inside. The two examples below illustrate the advantages of brevity.

> It has been brought to management's attention recently that many employees are using the fax machine and the Internet for reasons not necessarily pertaining to the normal conduct of business. For this reason, we are limiting the use of the fax machine and access to the Internet to those employees who are conducting business directly related to the carrying out of normal business transactions. (64 words)

> The fax machine and the Internet may be used for company business only.
> (13 words)

Next time you proofread a letter, pretend you are going to get $100 for every word you can eliminate. Do this on a regular basis and watch your word count decrease. You also will find your readers suddenly becoming more attentive.

A second and similar misconception in writing is that reminders are good. Some businesspeople write to co-workers as though they were communicating with forgetful scatterbrains.

"*The problems will remain the same, but apparently they get wordier and wordier.*'

> As we discussed this morning in my office when you
> and I met for coffee with Jim Jones . . .

Does the reader really need a recapitulation of the superficial details surrounding a recent conversation or decision? Or does he or she need to hear the same words repeated over and over, as in the following example?

> When change cards are submitted, most of the time
> the changes don't occur without a phone call; there-
> fore, make the change on the change card and then
> call your department superior and he will record the
> change.

(Yes, a businessperson actually wrote this.)

In many large organizations—especially in manufacturing companies, where few if any employees ever see the President or Chief Executive Officer—it is essential that all communications, whether interoffice memos or signs on bulletin boards, be written with the intended readers in mind.

Take the following example:

> With reference and regard to the matter that manage-
> ment has declared to be in the best interests of the fur-
> therance of company employee relations, the president
> has been authorized and empowered to grant each and

every employee, upon the attainment of 30 years of continued and uninterrupted service to the company and its aforementioned management, an additional period of vacation that shall be of one week's duration.

This 67-word obfuscation means simply that employees with 30 years' uninterrupted service will get an extra week's vacation.

When messages are wordy and redundant, filled with jargon and pretentious prose, not only are most people deterred from reading them, but those few who do take the time to read might not understand. Verbal camouflage can be costly.

Legal professionals, known for garrulousness, have an equal reputation for cleverness. As an example of the latter, the managing partner of a Baltimore law firm that specializes in maritime cases recently bragged to me about a time-saving "illustrated letter." Instead of discoursing at length about which party was at fault in a tugboat accident, he simply drew two pictures—one of the island, indicating the channel markers and the ships' courses, and another of the ship, showing where it was hit. Only a brief written explanation was attached. The clients were delighted with the simplification.

The truth is that lawyers often use too many words. It isn't always possible to substitute pictures for words, but with common sense it *is* always possible to avoid wordiness and redundancy.

Consider the following sentence, written by an attorney:

> In the event that any of the operations are located in facilities owned or occupied by one of the parties to the agreement, provision can be made for the allocation among the other members of rent, utilities and administrative support.

This unwieldy and strained 40-word sentence can be cut to 23 words and at the same time made clearer.

> Rent, utilities and administrative support can be allocated to members in facilities owned or operated by one of the parties to the agreement.

In the example below, legalistic long-windedness again gets in the way of clarity and economy.

> It should be pointed out that if the services to be performed by the Corporation were performed by a corporate entity that owned the underlying properties, the corporation probably could not elect Subchapter S treatment.
> (35 words)

Cartoon by John Spencer. Copyright © 2000 by John Spencer. Reprinted with permission of *Philadelphia Business Journal.*

Revised, the statement reads much more smoothly:

> If the corporate services were performed by a corporation that owned the properties, the corporation probably could not elect Subchapter S.
> (21 words)

The role of attorneys is to *assist* their clients—not to lead them blindfolded into a rhetorical maze. Some redundancies and clichés to avoid include *merging together, prior plans, several different, cooperate together, analyzes the question, comprehensive understanding, render inoperative, direct bearing, fiscal expenditures* and *cognizant awareness.*

Corporate lawyers have to be as vigilant as private practitioners. Businesspeople have little time to read dissertation-length communications; it is important to be brief.

Try this sample of tedious businessese:

> We have not made any announcement of our revision as we must write and file a new contract that will satisfy the readability requirements of the various states.
> (28 words)

The revision below is almost startling in its simplicity:

We will not announce our revisions until we file a new contract that satisfies state readability requirements.
(17 words)

Here's another time-consuming noncommunication:

It may well be that such management fees are not passive investment income and that the receipt of said fees would not count towards the 20 percent test.
(27 words)

And its possible revision:

If such management fees are not passive investment income, their receipt will not count toward the 20 percent test.
(18 words)

Then there's the reiterated question, which often irritates the reader who posed the question in the first place.

You have asked what effect, if any, these new laws will have upon fidelity bond operations.

The best solution is to avoid repeating the question and to proceed straight to the answer.

Finally, it's essential to know how to bow out. This can be done tediously:

> Once you have had an opportunity to review this letter, please contact me so that we can discuss how we should proceed in this matter. I look forward to hearing from you.
> (32 words)

Or briskness can rule:

> After you review the letter, please contact me.
> (8 words)

Wise Words: **To write more clearly and with greater economy, pretend that every word you use will cost $100.**

3

꒜

Meaningless Words and Awkward Sentences

I recently heard a vice president of a large consulting company tell a group that his firm "worked with the human element." Did the speaker imagine that his audience thought his firm worked with dogs or with monkeys? Don't all consultants—all businesspeople, in fact—work with other people? Unfortunately, too many of us are guilty—both in writing and in speaking—of producing meaningless words.

The same gentleman went on to say that he worked with "the human element as they transition." But *transition* is a noun meaning "a passage from one state or

"On the Internet, nobody knows you're a dog."

place to another"; it is not a verb. Therefore, people cannot "transition"; they can only "be in transition."

And even this improved wording begs the question: Transition from what, to what? Because I was already familiar with the speaker's company, I understood he meant to say that ABC Company helps people who have lost their jobs find new ones. Other listeners might have taken longer to catch on. His message would have been so much clearer if, instead of spouting meaningless words, he had explained in plain English that his company helps unemployed professionals find jobs.

Audiences are not impressed by meaningless words—"in a manner of speaking," "at this point in time," "sort of unique," "if I could possibly be of assistance in providing an opportunity to help," "as we move forward in our efforts"—expressions that confuse us, turn us off or put us to sleep.

People today have little time and less patience, so get to the point if you want readers and listeners. And forget the days when, as a high-school student wanting to impress your teachers, you kept a thesaurus next to your typewriter.

I recently received a letter requesting money for flood victims in the United States and displaced people in the Middle East, all of whom were caught in "conflictual situations." Although *conflictual* is a word—I looked it up in Webster's—why not just say "conflicts"?

When readers stumble over a wordy or awkward phrase, they automatically lose interest in the message, which defeats the writer's purpose.

Although words do not always communicate the messages intended, words often say a lot about the writer or speaker. Novelists rely on this principle to develop their characters. For example, in Jane Austen's *Pride and Prejudice,* when Mr. Collins says, "You may depend upon my not taking so material a step [as attending a ball given by an upper-class lady] without her ladyship's concurrence," the reader knows Collins is pompous. And when Jed, the drug dealer's mistress in John le Carré's *The Night Manager,* continually applies the adjective *super* to every situation and every person, the reader knows she's superficial.

One does not have to write a time-honored classic or a best-selling novel to sense how every word adds to or detracts from the overall message, and how it characterizes the writer or speaker. Indeed, a blank page— or a moment of silence—can be more effective than meaningless words.

Many years ago, when I was a girl in summer camp, if we weren't making lanyards or playing volleyball, we used to play a game called Telephone. Someone would whisper a word or phrase to her neighbor, who would in turn whisper what she had heard to her neighbor, until about 10 young campers had whispered messages to their neighbors seated in a circle.

Then the last person would announce what she had heard, which was always vastly different from what the original person had said.

In one of my recent writing workshops, as the participants tried unsuccessfully to figure out the meaning of the following sentence, I was reminded of this childhood game.

> In keeping with the exploratory paradigmatic nature of a pilot study, refinements to various operational aspects of the initiative evolved as a function of moderate experience in the field.

There had been no previous mention of a pilot study or any hint of this study's subject. Moreover, no one— including the writer, sad to say—could identify the "refinements," the "operational aspects," the "initiative," or the "field"; and as a result, no one could understand how the initiative had "evolved as a function of moderate experience in the field." Such gobbledygook at best forces readers to play silly guessing games, and at worst turns readers off—often for good.

Good writers never set up guessing games for their readers. They say exactly what they mean at all times. They use strong, concise topic sentences followed by specific descriptive and/or developing sentences, so that a busy reader is able to grasp information quickly and to decide whether or how to respond.

As managed care dominates healthcare delivery, liability issues become more important. For example, inaccurate diagnoses and record inconsistencies can be presented as evidence in a court of law.

The two sentences above, written by a lawyer to physicians, state and begin to explain a serious problem. There are no "initiatives," "aspects," "paradigms," "functions," or "explorations," but only specific nouns and adjectives for the reader to understand.

Indeed, writers should make every effort to use proper nouns—that is, names of specific persons, places or things—and should use only adjectives that describe nouns specifically and not those that merely enhance. For example, write "England's 17-percent value-added tax"—not "a country's average tax increase," which leaves the reader guessing.

Not many busy executives, lawyers, engineers and accountants have time to play Telephone. In every aspect of life—especially in business—words should be used to communicate a clear message and not simply to fill a page.

Wise Words: Could someone who does not share your professional knowledge easily understand what you have written? If not, go back and rewrite.

4

Jargon, Confusing Writing, Can't Masquerade As Style

Novelist Louis Auchincloss, who practiced law for many years, described jargon as "a disguise for mental apathy." For nearly every jargon word or phrase, there are half a dozen more precise and more effective equivalents. Nevertheless, many business and professional people mistakenly believe that the use of jargon signals sophistication.

When people talk about "modules and parameters," "utilizations and prioritizations," and "impacting" and "interfacing with" each other, they are spouting

gibberish that is meaningless even to others in their oc-
cupational group. When people interchange verbs,
nouns, and adverbs at will, they sound foolish to those
who know better. Why should passengers who exit an
Amtrak excursion train be said to "get off," whereas
those who leave the more expensive Amtrak Metroliner
are said to "de-train"? The would-be verb coined from a
noun is a blatant example of infatuation with jargon.

Another common example of jargon is the misuse
of *methodology* when *method* is meant. *Merriam Webster's
Collegiate Dictionary* (10th ed.) defines *methodology,* first,
as "a body of methods, rules, and postulates employed
by a discipline," and second, as "the analysis of the
principles or procedures of inquiry in a particular field";
whereas *method* is "a procedure or process for attaining
an object: as a systematic procedure, technique, or
mode of inquiry employed by . . . a particular discipline
or art." The same dictionary also lists three more definitions for *method,* followed by numerous synonyms—
such as *mode, manner* and *system.* Obviously, *method* is
the operative word in most cases, for accuracy as well as
conciseness. But because we are so accustomed to jargon, five syllables often seem better than two.

Other common examples of jargon involve misuse
of the words *parameters* and *paradigm.* Although the
word *parameters* pops up everywhere—in the post office
and the supermarket as well as on TV—I've yet to find a
writer in law or in business who can properly define it

"Sir, the following paradigm shifts occurred while you were out."

(perhaps because I haven't spoken to any mathematicians lately). According to *Merriam Webster's,* a parameter is "an arbitrary constant whose value characterizes a member of a system (as a family of curves); *also*: a quantity (as a mean or variance) that describes a statistical population." The second definition has to do with measuring "the temperature, pressure and density of the atmosphere." *Guidelines, categories, ramifications, limits* and *principles* are clearly not synonyms of *parameters.*

The first definition *Merriam Webster's* gives for *paradigm* is "an outstandingly *clear* [my italics] or typical example or archetype"; and the second is "an example of a conjugation or declension showing a word in all its inflectional forms." Yet those who use *paradigm* most often are not referring either to a linguistic chart or to an archetype.

The popular fascination with multisyllabic words and so-called ten-dollar phrases boggles the mind. I cringe every time I encounter *utilize* where *use* would do, *I am of the opinion* instead of *I believe, one is invited to* instead of *one should.* Ah, wordiness!

Just because a word sounds intellectual or impressive or lawyerly or vaguely familiar, doesn't make it right. The lawyer who wrote about "delivering a soliloquy" to a judge and jury obviously hadn't read *Hamlet* and didn't realize that a soliloquy is a monologue with an audience of one—the person speaking. Similarly, the lawyer who said he needed to "tame the Internet"—

"I'll start with the weekly progress report. For the benefit of new staff Ms. Snack, on my right, will act as acronym and jargon translator."

that is (again according to *Merriam Webster's*), "reduce [it] from a wild to [a] domestic state, make [it] docile or submissive"—was running amok with personification.

Misusers of language often combine the sublimely pretentious—*methodologies, paradigms, parameters*—with the ridiculously informal or slangy: legal actions that "knock out" state claims; exceptions that "swallow" rules; decisions that are "hashed out"; products that "hit" the marketplace; and "methodologies" that are "on a roll" and that will "leapfrog" the competition. All of these expressions sound silly and out of place in formal business and legal writing.

Once we understand why such wording is absurd, we can easily devise more precise, meaningful and grammatically correct words and phrases. And the better the writer's understanding of his or her subject, the easier it is to explain it.

Jargon is to be avoided primarily because it is vague and confusing. For example, when the boss tells an employee to perform a task "in a timely manner," does that mean next week, next month, early next year or tomorrow? Some tasks take months, even years, to accomplish, and others can be done in a day. The employee in this case would hardly be to blame if he or she took more time than the boss thought appropriate.

Secondly, jargon is undesirable because it tends to be wordy. *Pursuant to your request* and *in reference to your request* are superfluous; the recipient of your response presumably recalls the request that elicited it. *In a manner of speaking, in point of fact,* and *in the course of events* are other garrulous and meaningless expressions to be avoided. Likewise, *render inoperative* in most cases should be *stop*; *utilize* should be *use*; and *initiate* should be *start*. When two words have the same meaning, the shorter word is preferable.

Thirdly, jargon should be avoided because it is often grammatically incorrect. *Impact,* for example, is frequently used erroneously as a transitive verb. If I write well, my words can have an impact on my readers, but my words cannot be said to impact them (that is, physically to impinge on them and inhibit their movement or to strike them forcefully). Too many résumés never make it to the hiring officer because the writer of the cover letter wants "to impact the company's bottom line." And what is a bottom line, anyway? These overused expressions are as vague as *in a timely manner.*

During his presidential campaign, Bill Clinton talked a lot about "growing the economy"—as though the economy, an inanimate object, could get taller or fatter or sprout roots. Some listeners found this phrase jarring because it substituted a nonstandard, transitive form of the verb *to grow* for the expected intransitive form: the economy is generally said to grow, not to be grown. Clinton might have said instead that he wanted to increase economic growth or that his goal was a growing economy. But perhaps he was consciously imitating businesspeople who routinely speak of "growing the company," in an attempt to flatter them and gain their trust and support. Another favorite phrase, "shrink the deficit," doesn't sound quite as bad, perhaps because the verb *to shrink* ordinarily can take a direct object—and perhaps because we really do need to shrink the deficit.

Granted, language must evolve over time to accommodate new and different devices and ideas. Remember the noun *facsimile*? The advent of machines permitting the electronic transfer of facsimiles gave rise to a new noun with a more specific meaning *(fax)* as well as to the verb *to fax*. But if we care about communicating clearly, we will avoid the arbitrary interchange of different parts of speech, and of words with vastly different definitions, tones and contexts.

Users of jargon often sound silly and their messages are incomprehensible. Jargon is no substitute for simple, well-thought-out language. The best communicators in business and the professions, the best writers in literature and the sciences, use language that is concise and precise. Readers pay attention to their messages, and those messages often bring the desired results.

Wise Words: **Skip the jargon.**

5

Good Grammar Is Essential to Good Writing

Sixty years ago H. L. Mencken thought nothing of writing an editorial that covered an entire page of newsprint. And his readers clamored for more. Today fewer people read newspapers, books and magazines, and as a result, many don't know the difference between good and bad writing.

One hears discussions about legal writing, technical writing, scientific writing and business writing—as though each were a specific language, like German, Italian, Arabic or Greek. Law, technology, science and finance are subject areas, not adjectives defining a particular language or mode of writing.

There is *good* writing—about law and science and technology and lots of other subjects—and there is *bad* writing about the same subjects; and there are countless variations in between.

There are hundreds of possible mistakes in grammar and usage. Here are some of the most common and most irritating errors that professionals and businesspeople make.

1. CONFUSION OF PRONOUNS

Objective Versus Subjective Personal Pronouns

One cannot give something to *I* or work for *she.* Yet how many times do people write or say "It is between he and I" or "They gave it to John and I." Unlike German, Latin, Spanish and other languages, English has only two cases: subjective and objective.

The subjective pronouns—*I, he, she, we* and *they*—normally come at the beginning of a sentence, the subjective part. Objective pronouns—*me, him, her, us* and *them*—come after a preposition (*to, for, from, between, against* and so on) in the objective part, usually the second part of the sentence. Not very complicated if one knows the rule.

Examples: I am sharing the subject/object rule with him, with her, with them.

He, she, they should be grateful to me for sharing this information.

Relative Pronouns: Who and That

A second common pronoun error is the confusion between *who* and *that*. It is always *people who* and *things that*. Once again, a simple distinction—if one knows the rule.

Example: I hope the people who read this book will produce writing that is clearer and more grammatical.

2. THE *AFFECT/EFFECT* DILEMMA

To affect is a verb that means "to influence."

Example: I hope this chapter will affect and improve people's writing skills.

Effect is a noun that means "a result, consequence or outcome."

Example: The effects of good writing include new clients and customers.

But *effect* also can be used as a verb, meaning "to bring about, to cause to happen."

Example: A good writing workshop can effect a positive change in writing skills.

3. PRONOUNS AND APOSTROPHES

It's and Its

It's means "it is," whereas *its* indicates possession. There are no such words as *its'* and *our's*. Remember that an apostrophe after any pronoun always means "is."

> **Example:** It's not in your best interests to try to change its [the court's] decision.

Their, There, They're

Their is possessive: their briefs, their proposals. *There* is a place: put the briefs there, on the desk. *They're* is a contraction of the words *they are*.

> **Example:** They're going to put their briefs and memos over there.

4. PRONOUNS AND GENDER

The sentence "A person should help *their* company" may be socially acceptable, but it is grammatically flawed. Either say *"People* should help *their* companies" [plural] or

"*A person* should help *his* or *her* company." To avoid *he/she* or *her/him,* switch to the plural forms *they* and *them.* But if you use *they* or *them,* be sure also to use the plural form of the noun: *employees, people, individuals.*

5. LEARN AND RESPECT THE PARTS OF SPEECH

A *noun* is a person, place or thing. A *verb* is a word of action or a state of being. Nouns and verbs cannot be interchanged at will.

One cannot *impact, flowchart, wardrobe* or *team.* But one can *make an impact, use a flowchart, choose a wardrobe* or *form a team.* If writers want their readers to understand and take them seriously, then writers must express themselves correctly.

Similarly, adjectives can only modify nouns. No one can do something "real well," because *well* is an adverb, and only adverbs can modify other adverbs; so it must be "really well." When readers are brought up short by a grammatical error, they not only lose the narrative flow but they also lose the writer's message.

6. TENSE: SUBJECT AND VERB MUST AGREE

It is disconcerting to hear journalists, politicians or so-called intellectual talk-show hosts say "There is lots of possibilities," "There has been two occurrences," or "Numerous possibilities exists for change." Proper

English grammar dictates that subject and verb must always agree.

> **Examples:** There are many possibilities to express the many ideas that exist.
>
> There have been too many mistakes in grammar that when made in public affect each and every person.

7. A QUESTIONABLE WORD

The use of *hopefully* to mean "it is hoped," according to grammar books, should be avoided. Although it has gained wide acceptance, this dubious usage is not only grammatically incorrect; it also sounds tentative and frightened. It does not project the confident, positive image that professionals and businesspeople cultivate.

8. THE QUANTITY QUANDARIES

Between or Among

The correct usage is *between* two, but *among* three or more.

Less or Fewer

Use *fewer* for plural nouns that can be counted numerically: fewer people, professions, hours. Use *less* for nouns that cannot occur in the plural form and cannot be counted, as when referring to amount or extent: less time, butter, diplomacy.

9. THE TONE WORDS

Fine distinctions of tone and meaning can be crucial to the image a writer is trying to project. Following are two examples of paired synonyms that are often used interchangeably by those who are unaware of their different connotations.

Eager and Anxious

Eager means you are looking forward positively, with enthusiasm, to an event; *anxious* means you are scared, nervous or uptight about it.

Feel and Believe

One feels literally with one's hands and figuratively with one's heart, but one believes in one's mind. Obviously, the latter word is more appropriate in business and professional communications.

10. NUMBERS

The simple rule that appears in many grammar guides is: Numbers under 10 are written out—four, five, nine;

10 and above are written as numbers—12, 13 and so on, except when they begin a sentence.

Many other types of mistakes are possible in writing and speaking. We can err not only by using the wrong words but also by misusing the right words. During an episode of A Prairie Home Companion, Garrison Keillor once introduced a dog that growled every time he heard a grammatical error. In real life, unfortunately, most businesspeople and professionals must become their own watchdogs and growl at their own work. The ability to correct one's own mistakes—to catch the culprits, so to speak—could be the difference between retaining or losing a client, a grant or even a job.

Wise Words: **Keep the** *Harbrace Handbook* **or another good grammar text on your desk.**

6

꒜

Punctuation
and Transitions

Stage Directions
for the Reader

Although the marks of punctuation are small, the damage done when those marks are misused can be enormous. Vastly different meanings can be produced by varying punctuation, as illustrated by the following anecdote, which has circulated widely on the Internet:

> Male and female college students were told to provide punctuation for the sentence "Woman without her

man is nothing." The men wrote, "Woman, without her man, is nothing." The women wrote, "Woman: without her, man is nothing."

When readers see commas, they automatically pause, which is why I refer to commas as stage directions. They tell the reader what to do.

Example: As best I know, these receptions are also successful, I am eager to hear the Board's opinion.

The first comma is appropriate. The second should be a semicolon; you are separating two complete clauses.

The two most sensible comma rules are:

1. A comma indicates a short pause or a slight separation of ideas. Say the sentence to yourself. If there's a break, there's a comma. No break, no comma.
2. When in doubt about using commas, leave them out.

A dash—a line the length of two hyphens with no space between them—indicates a slightly longer pause or a greater separation of ideas than provided by a comma. Use a dash when you really want the reader to digest a brief aside.

"Why is it that every time I say something in
quotation marks you respond in italics?"

Parentheses should be used mainly to acknowledge supporting information—for example, definitions of acronyms and abbreviations, or citations of previous legal cases or judgments.

Quotation marks should be used only when quoting someone or referring to the title of a story or article, a song or a poem. They are not to be used to excuse jargon or slang, which should be avoided. A most important rule to remember, if you work in the United States, for an American-owned company or for the American branch of an international firm, is that the comma and the period *always* go *inside* the quotation marks; the bigger marks—that is, the colon and the semicolon—go outside. In the United Kingdom, Australia and all former British colonies, the comma and the period go outside the quotation marks.

Exclamation marks should be avoided in business and professional writing. The wording itself should relay the excitement. Whenever I see an exclamation point in business correspondence, I am reminded of the signs in television studios, prompting viewers to applaud or laugh on cue. The implication is that the performance is not entirely convincing on its own merits. If the writing is good, such stage directions are unnecessary.

Transitional words—*however, consequently, therefore, nevertheless* and so on—are a means of getting smoothly from one idea to another and showing the relationship between the ideas. (The Latin prefix *trans-*

means "across.") Transitional words, when used as stage directions for the reader, enhance readability and sophistication.

There is nothing wrong with the following paragraph, read without the bracketed words, except that it fails to provide a road map or stage directions for the reader.

> ABC and its former employees are classic outsiders insofar as running the business of DEF and its partners. [Specifically] There is no allegation that ABC or any of its former employees were officers, directors, or employees of DEF and its partners. [Moreover] ABC maintained entirely separate offices in a different state from DEF and engaged in an independent consulting relationship.

Now read the paragraph again, this time including the bracketed words. Can you tell the difference? Transitional words and phrases such as *instead, indeed, accordingly, therefore, nevertheless, on the other hand, primarily*—even *interestingly, obviously* or *unfortunately*—help the reader more easily absorb material that is otherwise tedious. Transitions also give the lawyer/writer a chance to editorialize, to express an opinion—which, in many cases, is what the client is paying for.

Without transitions, the reader has to work harder to interpret the message and to understand how the main points are connected. Witness the following series of nonspecific, staccato sentences.

I was hired and started my job. My knowledge came only from books. I was not prepared for the difficult period of adjustment. I soon became discouraged and was ready to quit. My employer must have known this. He asked me to come into his office. He talked to me about my work and about his. I realized there was nothing wrong with me or my new career. I decided to stay.

By strengthening the topic sentence, by adding some specific facts, by combining sentences and adding transitions, a writer can change that pedestrian, choppy paragraph into an interesting story.

In October 2001, three weeks after I was hired by Olmstead, Eager and Ernest, I realized that my knowledge of the law had come only from textbooks and that I was not prepared to research specific cases, to deal with clients or to work long hours. As a result, I became discouraged and even considered quitting. But Chip Smith, the partner to whom I was assigned, must have known how I felt. He invited me into his spacious corner office, where he offered me latte and bagels and told me about his first year as an associate at OE&E. In addition, he complimented me on my research on the Dominican Republic narcotics case. I then realized there was nothing wrong with me, and I decided to stay at OE&E.

Wise Words: Reread your writing, making sure it *flows.*

7

Active Versus Passive Voice
Who Is Responsible?

"Mistakes were made." How many politicians have you heard repeat those three words? Translated, they mean "I don't know who was responsible"—or perhaps more truthfully, "I don't want anyone to know that I was responsible."

Business and professional people should never indulge in vague communications. Unless your goal is to obfuscate, divert and stymie, you should always make clear who or what is responsible for the action you describe. Change passive, awkward-sounding sentences to active ones, as in the following examples.

> *Passive:* One million dollars of ABC life insurance was sold to a client by Shirley Jones.
> *Active:* Shirley Jones sold one million dollars of ABC life insurance.

> *Passive:* Announcement was made in President Clarke's letter of March 20, 2000, concerning various improvements in our Benefit Plan.
> *Active:* On March 20, 2000, President Clarke announced improvements to our Benefit Plan.

> *Passive:* In accordance with your request, several samples are enclosed.
> *Active:* I am enclosing several samples.

> *Passive:* The motion was passed by the delegates unanimously.
> *Active:* The delegates unanimously passed the motion.

> *Passive:* Several program source listings were reviewed.
> *Active:* We reviewed several program source listings.

When an accountant tells a client, "It is suggested that you put $10,000 in an account to minimize taxes," the client may or may not act as counseled. But when the accountant advises, "Put $10,000 in an account to minimize taxes," the client knows what he or she *must* do.

In business, one cannot afford to sound wishy-washy. Strong executives say what they mean—in the active voice. Here are two more examples that are passive and wordy, followed by clearer, active variants.

> *Passive:* An inventory of unprocessed items should be made by actual count and entered in the appropriate space on the form.
> *Active:* Inventory unprocessed items and enter them on the form.

> *Passive:* The report should be submitted to Terrence Baker.
> *Active:* Submit your report to Terrence Baker.

Professional and businesspeople who write awkward, wordy and indirect—that is, passive—sentences often do so in the mistaken belief that this is typical professional style. The following awkward construction of 23 words does not equate with appropriate legal writing style. It is merely bad writing. In contrast, the edited version of five words shown afterward is clear and concise. This is good writing about the law.

> *Before:* With respect to the handgun industry, rather it is the result of actions taken by third parties which renders them instrumentally dangerous.
>
> *After:* Third-party actions make guns dangerous.

Scientific writing is challenging even for scientists. Most scientists spend a good part of their lives in their laboratories, performing experiments. But unless they can communicate their results properly and concisely, their endless hours may be wasted.

In the example below, 21 poorly used words guaranteed to confuse any reader have been whittled down to eight words sure to inform. Is the 21-word statement an example of scientific writing? Hardly. Just poor writing.

> *Before:* Once that sample is obtained, we are trying to make decisions about it, because that is what we are targeted to.
>
> *After:* After we get the sample, we will decide.

Some wordy sentences, even if rewritten, serve no purpose. The next example, which contains 31 words, is superfluous and should simply be deleted.

The purpose of this letter is to identify and request support for ABC requirements for test data needed to comprehensively test the ABC software that will be delivered to the UK.

(If your letter contains the ABC requirements for test data, that fact should be self-explanatory.)

Again, these examples should not be taken as evidence that technical writing is inevitably redundant and boring. They mean only that the writer hasn't taken the time to read what he or she has written to see whether it makes sense.

Is it active or passive, good or bad writing? Those are the questions that matter.

Wise Words: **Begin nearly every sentence with a strong subject and verb. Make it active. Take responsibility.**

8

Structure
and Organization
The Formula for Success

Wouldn't it be lovely if each of us had a muse sitting in a cage behind us, inspiring us to write wonderful prose? When reports and briefs, memoranda and proposals, must be written for a deadline, we cannot wait to be inspired by muses or by anything else. We must keep writing.

But then, on the second or third page, we should *stop*, read, and find the *strong, active topic sentence*. That's where communication should begin. The key to good organization is logical paragraph structure. Every good paragraph contains:

1. A topic sentence;
2. One, two, or three descriptive and/or developing sentences; and
3. A concluding (if it's just one paragraph or the last paragraph) or transitional sentence (when other paragraphs follow it).

In many instances, (3) can be (2); that is, a descriptive and/or developing sentence also can serve as a concluding or transitional sentence.

The more time that lawyers spend researching and writing briefs, memoranda, letters and other documents, the more they need to remember that they are writing for readers other than themselves. Clients, judges and other lawyers quickly lose patience when they must peruse pages and pages of a brief, memorandum or letter before getting to the point. Remember the advice I gave in Chapter 2: Economize on words.

Few look to legal writing for entertainment; and those who must read lawyers' writing have short attention spans because of constant pressures and demands on their time. They therefore have little patience for reading something that is not concise, that does not state the facts up front and that lacks a strong topic sentence at the beginning of each paragraph.

A good writer puts the reader on the scene and carefully involves him or her in the story or message, as in the following example:

> On March 4, 2002, at 9:50 A.M., a hyperactive Boston terrier, owned by Jefferson R. Pringle III, CEO of Pringle Ltd., took a large bite out of my client's leg, tearing to shreds his tailor-made Armani suit, and thereby preventing him from addressing his annual stockholders' meeting scheduled for 10 A.M.

Unfortunately, however, most legal briefs contain material that is neither humorous nor interesting; instead, they typically begin like this:

> Upon grievances filed by ABC International Union of North America, Local 2000 (hereinafter "Union") under its collective bargaining agreement with Sullivan County, N.Y. (hereinafter "County"), a hearing was held before the Arbitrator on May 10, 1998, in Sullivan County, N.Y. Testimony was adduced and exhibits were introduced. A transcript of the hearing was not made at that point in time. This post-hearing brief is filed pursuant to leave granted by the Arbitrator.

Actually, as legal briefs go, this is not a bad start; but the topic sentence is weak, and more specific information should be included. Who held the hearing, and for how many grievances? What testimony was taken, and what sorts of exhibits were introduced? By eliminating the passive voice (e.g., instead of "a hearing was held," by writing "Judge Jones held a hearing") and by deleting empty phrases such as "at that point in time," the writer could have given the reader pertinent facts with fewer words.

No matter what a lawyer or any other businessperson writes, he or she must tell a story to engage the reader. And the more esoteric the topic, the more interestingly that story must be told. To hold the reader's interest, every paragraph must be well organized, beginning with a strong, specific topic sentence. Do not begin a paragraph with a statement like this:

> This letter should provide my deliberate comments and questions on whether the merger between ABC and DEF can withstand legal challenge.

Instead, get to the heart of the matter:

> According to California Statute 999, ABC can merge with DEF by December 21, 2002, with the following three [brief] provisions.

Don't begin a paragraph with:

This memorandum is based on general information on which we are relying, obtained for the most part from our independent research using publicly available information.

Instead, give the reader facts:

The patent application for cancer cure 007 has been rejected by the FDA, which considered 15 percent of the animal research inaccurate.

Then follow with specific examples that support the topic sentence. For example:

The dye used to determine the extent of cell blockage in the control group of rats had been diluted with alcohol.

It is the writer's responsibility to assist the reader and the lawyer's responsibility to assist the client. Without a strong, specific topic sentence in the beginning of a document and in subsequent paragraphs, the reader will not know what the writer is trying to communicate. Without descriptive sentences that support the topic sentence by providing examples, the reader will not have the necessary specifics. Without smoothly flowing sentences, the reader will lose interest. In the

United Kingdom, a period is called a full stop. Give your readers too many full stops, and they will.

Wise Words: In organized paragraphs:

1. The topic sentence makes a strong statement.
2. The topic sentence is followed by a sentence that *could* begin with "for example"—even if you don't begin it with those words.
3. A good paragraph usually contains at least two or three interrelated sentences and does not ramble.

9

Striking the Right Tone

The *tone* of a letter or memo is the overall attitude conveyed by the writer's words. Letters and memos can sound melodious or cacophonous, interesting or boring, depending on how they are composed.

Whether the writer believes the reader (the boss, co-worker or client) is brilliant, stupid, immature, cheap or difficult is often betrayed by tone. Therefore, business writers generally attempt to conceal negative feelings about the people to whom they are writing to achieve the desired results. In business and the professions, tone is often a barometer of the degree of success or failure a writer has with customers and clients.

Naturally, in a sales letter tone is very important. An officious or wishy-washy tone is not going to make a reader want to buy your product. Knowledge, sincerity and enthusiasm are what you want to express.

For example, if you are introducing a new product or service to a middle-aged client you have never met, you would not write, "Hey John Boy, wait till you hear about the new XYZ Widget. You just can't beat it." But if John is a young, creative type, or a friend as well as a current client, that introduction might be fine.

The tone of follow-up letters is important too. You don't want to insult a client who has neglected to pay a bill. But on the other hand, you don't want to appear too mild-mannered, or your firm may never receive the money the client owes.

Regrettably, many people who work for companies in which client relationships are paramount—especially service industries, such as engineering, architecture, accounting and law—write like the Internal Revenue Service:

Per your request, enclosed please find . . . . [Reader's interpretation: "It's there, dummy; if you look for it, you'll find it."]

Instead, write, "I am happy to enclose the ABC materials you requested."

Although rumor has it that the IRS is trying to soften its unfriendly image, IRS agents do not really look forward to meeting any of the thousands of citizens who receive its notices. However, in a client-driven company, one must make friendly personal contact. Here's another example:

ABC Company presents the following information. [Reader's interpretation: "ABC says, 'Take it or leave it.'"]

Instead, you could write, "We at ABC are delighted to share with you the following information."

It can be difficult to strike an appropriate tone, as evidenced by the examples below, written by lawyers. Most criticisms of lawyers' writing are focused on their belabored overuse of coordinating conjunctions such as *heretofore, henceforth, insofar as* and *herein.* But a much more subtle problem with lawyers' language, especially in letters, is that of tone. It is one thing to put the fear of God into a witness in the courtroom or into a colleague or subordinate in a boardroom; it is quite another to use that tone when writing to a recalcitrant client. Being sensitive—that is, using a courteous tone—is never a weakness. It is a more effective way of dealing with people.

Consider the following letter to a young foreign student, written by an associate in a prestigious law firm.

Dear Ms. Suzuki:

This letter confirms our January 6 discussion. At that meeting you decided not to seek an extension of your student visa. Instead, you insisted you plan to continue your unauthorized employment and try to seek permanent-resident status through marriage to an American citizen. I believe that the course you have chosen exposes you to the threat of deportation. We will be able to do little for you should you attract the attention of the INS. I remind you that although we have ceased work on your behalf, you remain obligated to pay our fees on schedule. Therefore, you must continue to remit $– per week. If you question this letter or rethink your current decision, you can call me.

The staccato sentences, the vague but detectable threats, and the clinical and distant tone in this letter would alienate the client. Note the substantial change in tone in the following revision.

Dear Ms. Suzuki:

When we met on January 6, you decided not to extend your student visa but to continue working and perhaps to get married. I am concerned because I believe that without a visa extension, you may be subject to deportation. If the INS finds you, I am afraid there will be little I can do. Although you are not presently a client, you still owe us $–. I therefore look forward to receiving your weekly $– until the bill is paid. If you have any questions, or if you change your mind about the visa, please do not hesitate to call me.

What does one do about a wealthy client who doesn't pay bills on time, or who questions the amount and value of the work you have performed? The tone of the following lawyer's letter certainly will not help in this situation.

Dear Dr. Alexander:

I trust your recent trip to Spain and Italy was a pleasant one. As I told you on the telephone this past Friday, I am enclosing a copy of the First Codicil to your Last Will and Testament and our invoice for our professional services rendered with respect to the preparation of this Codicil. The amount of this invoice is in excess of the amount we estimated when we began because of the numerous changes made to the Codicil after your marriage. Insofar as these changes were necessitated by revisions in your testamentary desires, we believe it seemingly appropriate to bill you for them. To the extent that revisions were made as a result of our error, no additional change has been made.

I am fully aware that you have objected to our billing practices in the past. For this reason, we have been scrupulous in allocating new work to the

enclosed First Codicil. If you have any questions con-
cerning this allocation, please feel free to contact me,
and I will gladly review our computerized time sheets
with you.

Not only is the letter excessively wordy, but the defen-
sive tone is inappropriate for a business letter. The mention of Dr. Alexander's apparently extensive vacation to
Spain and Italy seems snide, patronizing and unnecessary, as does the reference to his new wife. The calling of
attention to possible legal errors (were such errors made,
or not?), the intimation that less care might have been
given to earlier work than to work more recently completed, and the allusions to Dr. Alexander's objections
to previous bills are likely to add fuel to the client's ire.

The revision is both more direct and more cordial:

Dear Dr. Alexander:
Enclosed with our invoice is a copy of the First Codicil
to your Last Will and Testament. Because you requested a number of changes in the Codicil, our
charges are more than I had originally anticipated.
Nevertheless, we have been careful in allocating new
work to the enclosed Codicil. If you have any questions, please call me. I will be happy to discuss how I
arrived at this amount.

The tone of a business letter should be appropriate, courteous and nonthreatening throughout. If *how* one communicates—rather than *what* one communicates—gives a letter's recipient the wrong impression, the writer is responsible.

Wise Words: Reread your correspondence before you send it, imagining yourself in the recipient's place. Then make appropriate changes.

10

~

Poor Writing
Is Not Style

Gibberish? Bad writing? No. "That's my style!"

The word *style,* so often misused, is defined by *Webster's New Collegiate Dictionary* (8th ed.) primarily as "a mode of expressing thought in language." A secondary definition that also pertains to writing is "the manner or method of acting or performing, especially as sanctioned by some standard."

Standard is indeed the operative word defining style; and in business, as elsewhere, the standard for writing style is excellence, measured in terms of clarity and effectiveness. Business writing affects the daily lives of all employers, customers and workers as it influences the flow of goods and services and profits.

Therefore, it is most unfortunate when an engineer writes, "In the previous section we extended the knowledge state for such a two-state physical device to four states for the knowledge system variable representing machine belief about that device," and defends it as "my style"; or when a bank manager writes, "The procedure has as its objective at this point in time to clearly delineate responsibilities and consequently lessen the liability involved in this manual process," and answers the reader's question about what he means with "That's just my style." Bad writing cannot be equated with style, nor does "style" excuse it—especially in professional or technical fields, where writers bear an even greater responsibility to readers lacking their expertise.

Some read Shakespeare or Dostoyevsky or Henry James for edification or education; others read Tom Clancy or Mary Higgins Clark for entertainment. But in business, we all read to gather information and prepare for action. If you want readers to invest in your funds or to purchase your products or to agree with your ideas, you must be able to explain succinctly and convincingly what they will be investing in, buying or agreeing to. This is especially true in today's competitive marketplace, where people have many possible alternatives and tend to take their choices seriously.

Ernest Hemingway, while working as a reporter for the *Kansas City Star,* developed a clear, concise, clipped style that he later used to great effect in crafting timeless works of fiction. But those with the flair of a Hemingway are few and the percentage of businesspeople and lawyers who could follow in his footsteps—Michael Lewis, Scott Turow, Richard North Patterson, Linda Fairstein and a few others—is minuscule. It is therefore naive for trainers, managers and continuing education specialists to constantly emphasize style.

The only "style" needed in business writing is clarity, conciseness and impeccable organization. Business writing should not be wordy or redundant, awkward or jargon-filled. It should contain no errors in sentence structure, usage, grammar or punctuation. Lastly, the tone should be polite and consistent.

Creativity—which has so often been used as an excuse for substandard style—should be left to those who, like the modern writers mentioned above as well as Hemingway the newspaper correspondent, Wallace Stevens the insurance agent, and Herman Melville the bureaucrat, were outstanding business communicators before they became crafters of timeless fiction and poetry.

Wise Words: **In business, style and creativity may abound, while good writing is a rarity that must be cultivated.**

PART TWO

Words on Marketing

Introduction

Once upon a time, there was one local grocery and one local department store, one local car dealer and one local telephone service. There also was a local lawyer who could handle almost any transaction and a local accountant who could do the same. Many people who are reading this book won't remember such a time, but trust me, reader—it did exist.

Nowadays, monopolies are anathema. Just look at what happened to AT&T and what is happening to Microsoft. Law firms are reconfiguring and sprouting up everywhere. Some are conglomerates; others are boutiques. It is the same with accounting firms. First, it was the Big Eight, then the Big Six. Now it is individual name recognition that counts.

Competition in business is supposedly good for the customer, the consumer. But for manufacturers, sellers and consultants (i.e., lawyers, accountants, bankers, insurers, physicians, engineers, architects and others)—for virtually every business owner, large or small—successful competition today requires skillful marketing to both internal and external clients. Marketing has become a billion-dollar-a-year industry.

Marketing depends mostly on communication, especially on good writing skills. Excellent communication can help a company enormously; poor communication can hurt or even destroy it.

11

Writing to Market
Creating an
Outstanding Sales Brochure

Like many businesspeople who often travel out of state, I rely on a particular car service to get to and from the airport. Recently, while driving me home from the airport in a new Lincoln Town Car, John (not his real name), who owns the service I use and who employs at least a dozen drivers (all college-educated, friendly and efficient), explained that *he* often drives during the five o'clock rush hour because that is the toughest shift. *Hmm,* I thought, not only is John punctual and efficient but he also shoulders the workload alongside his employees. He is a great boss and his company provides outstanding service.

And then he gave me a copy of his company's new brochure—a foldout in two colors, with eight panels of solid type. Most of the text seemed redundant and negative, emphasizing the various mishaps that might affect drivers and passengers—from foul weather to changing flight schedules to rush-hour traffic. No fewer than seven times, the brochure explained how to reach the driver (specifying the same phone number each time) should he or she fail to arrive at the appointed hour. Adding insult to injury, the text was marred by mistakes in sentence construction and in punctuation.

Having used several car services in the past 20 years, and having heard war stories from friends and business associates who also regularly use such services, I *know* this one is outstanding. But would anyone be able to tell that from its brochure?

Unfortunately, many marketing brochures, whether created internally or externally, do not accurately represent the companies they are supposed to promote; ironically, some so-called marketing brochures even deter potential customers. Although many company owners do an outstanding job, offer excellent services and products and hire efficient people, most are unable to describe their accomplishments in writing—which is why hiring a top-notch marketing professional is so important.

"I write astronaut banter for NASA."

The artistic design of a brochure certainly matters, but the text—that is, the writing—says it all. Here are some critical questions to ask yourself when putting together or evaluating your company's brochure.

1. *Who will read it?* This is the most important question. Most busy executives do not have time to read more than is necessary. Keep the text short and simple, and avoid repetition. There is nothing wrong with white space used judiciously, as part of an attractive design.

2. *How educated are my clients/readers?* In the case of this particular car service, the correct answer is "very." And educated readers are turned off by mistakes in grammar, usage and punctuation. In contrast, everyone appreciates good writing—even if not everyone can produce it.

3. *How can I best accentuate the positive?* Traffic may be snarled, planes may be late, and weather may be unpredictable, but these are exceptions, and every frequent traveler knows this. When describing your valuable product to prospective buyers, you need not tell them when, how and why it may fall apart. Simply deal with problems fairly and resourcefully *if and when* they arise. A marketing brochure should not scare away potential customers.

4. *What are the three most important qualities of my service or product that distinguish me from my competition?* It's okay to list fewer than three, but more than three is overkill. In the case of the car service, such assets may be

the youth, education/intelligence and physical strength of the drivers—characteristics guaranteed to reassure up-scale retirement-complex dwellers who need someone to carry their luggage as well as to carry on an intelligent conversation all the way from Baltimore County, Maryland, to Kennedy International in New York.

5. *How can I best boast about my business?* Use appropriate and interesting testimonials. It makes more sense to let a satisfied client toot your horn than to toot it yourself. If Mrs. Jones, a retired school principal living at Blakehurst, says good things about her car service, then Dr. Brown of Charlestown is apt to try it. Similarly, if the CEO of a major company in Owings Mills explains why he uses the service, then the COO of a large company in Hunt Valley might well choose it as the preferred mode of travel for all company executives.

No one knows your business better than you do. Therefore, only you can best define it. A good marketing writer should know this and work with you to reveal the unique aspects of your business, helping you create a truly effective sales and marketing brochure.

Wise Words: **Never underestimate the importance of a first-rate marketing brochure.**

12

Writing Your Firm's Future

It may be a good idea to rely on first-rate marketing and public relations people to publicize a business like the car service described in the previous chapter, but what if your company is a law firm or a sci-tech start-up that provides highly specialized services?

Some firms rely exclusively on marketing and public relations people to promote their products or services. Although they may be good writers, these people usually are not lawyers and they may not know much about the legal profession. It may be more effective for lawyers who have been through a focused writing and editing workshop to write their own articles and brochures describing their specialties and their experiences working on particular cases.

Although a poorly written article in a trade paper or magazine actually can harm a firm, a well-written article that includes specific and relevant examples can be worth its weight in gold. Especially in complicated areas of the law—intellectual property, patent infringement, environmental protection, product liability and licensing, intricate corporate mergers and acquisitions—well-written articles can attract new and exciting clients.

I still remember reading one lawyer's poorly written article on a real estate transaction. The writer provided a somewhat muddled history followed by a boring description of the intricacies of the transaction. Moreover, this lawyer never thought of using the specific example of a real person who had gone through such a transaction and had emerged unscathed and significantly richer. Journalists call the technique "putting the reader on the scene"; lawyers might call it *in medias res.* If readers can identify with someone in your article and see how that person's problems were solved and how they themselves might also benefit from hiring you—monetarily and in other ways—you can bet they will call you.

Nearly all large law firms today also produce marketing brochures. True, a picture is worth a thousand words, but unless the text is as clear as the photographs, the brochure will not succeed in its primary mission: attracting new business. Again, the public relations writers who are often hired to produce brochures are not lawyers, and even the best PR writers often need editors. Therefore, it is essential that all lawyers at a firm, from senior partners on down through the ranks, understand what makes first-rate writing.

Although writing is a consistently underrated skill and a task often relegated to first-year associates, excellent writing can help a firm excel and prosper in all it does—especially in projecting a professional image.

Wise Words: Lawyers, create your own marketing brochures and articles whenever possible.

13

Writing a Winning
Proposal or Business Plan

The most difficult marketing pieces to write may well be the proposal, grant application and business plan. What the writer must do is convince potential investors to back a product or service or research that may not yet be fully developed.

Having a great plan or a product that will change technology or save lives is important. But cogently communicating to potential investors your idea or product or service is even more important. And even people with excellent backgrounds in science and technology may lack the communication skills needed to convince potential investors to sponsor them.

Hiring a professional proposal writer may be a popular choice, but it is not always the best choice. Only *you* fully understand your idea, research or product, and see its potential. Therefore, only you can transmit your enthusiasm for its development to others. If you can attend a high-quality workshop to hone your writing skills, that is the best way to go. But in case you can't, here are some tips you can use to evaluate and improve your own writing.

1. *Organization.* The first paragraph in a proposal is the most important. Busy readers cannot go searching for clues. Therefore, the first paragraph (and every paragraph after it) should begin with a *strong topic sentence,* followed by one to three descriptive sentences elaborating that topic.

2. *No jargon.* Proposal readers are instantly put off by jargon and empty phrases. Avoid "in a timely manner," "stimulating concept," "bottom line," "burning questions," "warrants further investigation," "resource utilization," "real challenges" and so on. Instead, state in clear, well-thought-out language what is *special* about *your* proposal.

"Now, now, Ruffy, if you'll spare me the threats
I'll spare you the legal jargon."

3. *Readability.* Involve your reader so that he/she wants to soak up every detail. To do this, you must avoid wordiness and redundancy, choppy sentences, awkward phrases and clichés. Your writing should *flow.*

4. Include *specific examples* and anecdotes to put your reader immediately in the picture.

5. Be *brief* and *concise.* If you can't say what you need to within a *few* pages, then it may not be worth saying at all.

Wise Words: **Write your own business plan if you can.**

PART THREE

A Few Words on Technology

14

Communicating
on the Internet

No book on writing in the 21st century would be complete without a discussion of the Internet, which may be the communication medium most widely used in business today. The Internet has its share both of admirers and of detractors, for its pervasive influence can be a curse as well as a blessing.

Colleges and universities consider the Internet a blessing because it places an unlimited amount of information at students' fingertips. Many professors believe they now need only teach their students to evaluate research, to organize it, and then to present it clearly and concisely. And because so many students use the Internet, English departments, which had been shrinking since the 1960s, have seen a greater demand for their services—namely, the teaching of good communication skills—even among non–English majors.

However, all information circulated on the Internet must be critically evaluated. Anyone can create an electronic document and post it on a web site. The source of the information must always be considered: is it trustworthy and authoritative?

Yet many users of the Internet—including professional and businesspeople—assume that if it says so on the screen, then it's gospel. A recent experience reported to me by a friend belies that assumption.

My friend had used the Internet to find out more about his ancestor and namesake, Raphael Semmes, a prominent figure in the Confederate Navy. The online encyclopedia indicated that Admiral Semmes had graduated from the U.S. Naval Academy in Annapolis; but in fact, Semmes became a naval officer before the Academy was even established. The information was inaccurate, perhaps due to the writer's carelessness.

Users of the Internet must be alert not only to the possibility of unintentional errors but also to that of disinformation—the deliberate circulation of inaccurate information with the goal of misleading others. Common examples include falsified résumés, fallacious stock market advice, and bogus services and products (for example, herbs that are said to cure cancer). Information of any kind can be put on the Internet at virtually no cost to its creator and regardless of its quality. Moreover, because the Internet allows the creators of misinformation and disinformation to communicate anonymously (or pseudonymously), it insulates them from the normal consequences of disseminating false or flawed information.

The advent of e-mail—which is in a communication class by itself—has encouraged just about everyone to try his or her hand at writing off-the-cuff, with little or no preparation or forethought. As a result, lawyers, architects, accountants—all businesspeople, in fact—have been given an equal opportunity to embarrass themselves.

E-mail tends to be rife with grammatical errors, tortured phrases, awkward usage, abbreviated spellings, incorrect punctuation (or no attempt at punctuation) and typographical errors. Unfortunately, e-mail also can be disseminated at the click of a button to a wide audience—often to the chagrin of the writer and his or her company.

E-mail, perhaps because it is so easy to produce and transmit, has led to a decline in the quality of internal communication. Following are a few examples typifying this trend.

Hi Janie I thought giving you a better understanding of the process that takes place in DOC when you request a 124 or 126 or any other claim to be pulled, would hopefully help keep things running smoothly for you.

Readers need to breathe, and punctuation allows them to do that. It also increases readability and clarity of meaning. Unfortunately, punctuation—in the above e-mail as well as in the next example—has practically disappeared.

Bob, Congratulations!! I talked to Jane Smith this afternoon and she advised that your effort in expanding the capacity to feed the export order by acquiring an [sic] automated billing equipment will be eligible for the grant you are awarded so please provide the information and all the receipts to us per as her instruction by March 9, 2002.

Even when inviting co-workers to an informal event, such as a company picnic, correspondence should be correct in both substance and style. Mistakes, whether in grammar, sentence structure or tone, reflect negatively on the writer and his or her company.

Working on the Internet in a relaxed environment—one's private office or home—often lulls users into a false complacency. Keep in mind that although your reader cannot see your bare feet, your jeans and T-shirt, she can spot your written mistakes. You may think that if it's not a letter, it doesn't really have to be correct. Not so. Even messages lacking the traditional logo and letterhead reflect on their sender and his or her company.

Because of the sloppiness of much solicited e-mail as well as the daily flood of unsolicited e-mail—jokes, advertisements, medical advice, crossword puzzles and stock tips—many businesspeople and professionals don't read their e-mail at all.

On the plus side, the Internet provides many benefits. At little or no cost, all Internet users have instant, worldwide exposure for their products, their services and their opinions. Sitting at one's desk at home or in a nearby office, one can communicate with the world. An e-mail message can be sent simultaneously to people on every continent. And in less than five minutes, a businessperson in Baltimore can send a message to a businessperson in Beijing and receive a response.

Moreover, the Internet has proven an outstanding research tool for lawyers in the past decade. Even before the Internet, lawyers began to rely on software programs such as Lexus-Nexus and WestLaw to access various databases during their legal research. But the Internet has virtually changed the practice of law in the 21st century in three ways.

First, the Internet provides access to extensive corporate directories. For example, a lawyer can access a company web site anywhere in the world and learn about its products, its manufacturing processes and its methods of distribution—practically its entire history.

Second, with a click of the mouse, a lawyer can check the status of almost any court case. Let's say an attorney has an appeal before the Fourth Circuit Court. At no financial cost, he can print out all opinions that this particular court has issued within the last five years. Incredibly, since all court filings are done on the Internet, one can check the status of any case currently before the courts.

Finally, by typing *antitrust* and *Microsoft* in a keyword search, for example, a lawyer can tap into an enormous amount of material. But depending on the specific case, the material may not be complete. Therefore, lawyers must be able to organize huge bodies of research, to condense, to simplify, to reorganize and to edit material into a form suitable for their readers—whether they are clients, judges, mediators or adversaries.

To be sure, the Internet provides vasts amounts of instant information, without its users having to go to a library or even to a mailbox. But the instantaneous communication provided by the Internet is a curse as well as a blessing. Let's say a businessperson comes home after an extraordinarily grueling day when everything that could have gone wrong went wrong. He or she sends the boss an e-mail message saying "I quit!" An hour later, having opened a batch of mortgage and credit card bills, this person realizes that this message was a dreadful mistake. But it's too late. The boss has already responded: "Resignation accepted."

Despite all the hype, the Internet is merely a tool operated by humans. In order to master it effectively, we must use our knowledge efficiently—that is, we must communicate properly and sensitively.

British commentators in the eighteenth century described letter writing as an art that at once informed, entertained and revealed the self. In the 21st century, communication in all forms and in all media still informs, entertains and reveals. It is up to us to determine how we reveal ourselves.

APPENDIX

More
Helping Words

A Business Is
Not a University

On-the-job training is important to businesspeople—from highly educated professionals to recent high school graduates working at the entry level. Not only does it give employees a chance to improve their skills and learn new ones, but it shows that the company cares about its employees' professional advancement and growth. Thus, training provides a practical as well as a psychological bonus.

But training, like anything, can be taken to extremes. Although on-site workshops related directly to participants' jobs are useful, the workplace is not a university. The university may educate people who join the workplace and successful companies may contribute monetarily to the university, but the workplace and the university are two distinct entities.

Nevertheless, some large companies seem bent on creating internal universities. Indeed, approximately 20 years ago, a well-known Fortune 500 company created and aggressively marketed a number of learning modules for the business workplace. But the modules often had little or nothing to do with workers' tasks; by the time they were developed, they were obsolete. Offering on-the-job, personalized training is a good idea; providing a huge menu of canned courses is not. For many reasons, companies cannot duplicate universities.

First, the best workplace educations are interactive. Modules and flashcards, lectures transmitted via the Internet, and other training tools that are generic or canned—that is, produced with the broadest possible audience in mind—won't enable an employee to deliver a better speech, prepare an intricate financial statement, win an argument or a bid, program a computer, operate a machine, write a proposal or supervise a group.

A successful businessperson is a participant in a group in which the members share and complement one another's skills, all working toward the good of the company—whether it be an architecture or law firm, a bank or a hospital. The formation of good working relationships is key to learning and professional growth. In contrast, the best university education is often solitary. If a student becomes involved in too many groups or goes to too many parties, there will not be enough time for research and study.

Second, successful students *take* what they can from the university—extra research, papers, tutorials and the like. Good grades are their external reward. Successful workers, on the other hand, *give* to their companies. Their paycheck is their external reward.

Moreover, whereas education is—or should be—central to students' lives, workers also find their jobs central. But unlike most students, most workers also have family responsibilities, making their outside-of-work time precious. They cannot be expected to do homework or to master abstract concepts or skills that are seemingly extraneous to what they do daily. The most successful education for workers takes place on the job.

Another difference between business and the university has to do with depth. The best universities provide a *broad* liberal arts education so that students gain a sense of history, a perspective that allows them to better appreciate and understand their surroundings and to build on a strong foundation. Fittingly, many organizations prefer workers with liberal arts backgrounds, who—as studies have shown—learn specialized tasks more quickly. Wall Street headhunters, for example, often prefer to hire liberal arts graduates, then teach them financial expertise on the job or encourage them to study for MBAs in their spare time. Similarly, whereas medical schools once selected only undergraduate science majors, during the past decade they have sought out liberal arts majors.

Several years ago, a popular British writer and former English professor, David Lodge, wrote a novel called *Nice Work*. In it, the male managing director of a large manufacturing company agrees to switch places with a female philosophy professor at a public university. Because their respective experiences in this turnabout are so different from what they expected, the book is often pathetic and humorous at the same time. Although each eventually learns something from having stood in the other's shoes, it is clear that their differences are still much greater than their commonalities.

Certainly both universities and businesses play important roles in people's lives. But the best universities and colleges have stuck to their missions—hiring the most qualified professors, offering the highest-quality courses, and providing the broadest possible educations not only for the world of work but also for public service and personal development. And the best businesses have continued to offer on-site, job-related, interactive training—and have not tried to become universities.

Wise Words: As Tom Peters wrote in *In Search of Excellence*, the timeless business best-seller, "The best companies stick to their knitting."

Evaluating a Writing Course or Workshop

Every consultant should provide an evaluation for participants to complete at the end of a workshop, including questions such as the following.

1. List several ways in which this workshop has helped improve your specific writing and editing skills [or whatever the workshop was designed to do].
2. Was the instructor knowledgeable and well-prepared?
3. Did you find the materials used in the workshop helpful?
4. Name two or three things that were especially helpful and explain why.

5. Would you recommend this workshop to others in your organization? Why or why not?

This type of evaluation should elicit a response that will be informative and helpful both to the consultant and to the firm or company.

However, other signs also can and should be used to evaluate results. First, are the workshop participants forming informal buddy systems? Are they reviewing each other's writing before it goes out?

Second, are group follow-up sessions taking place in the organization, led by a department head or a partner? For example, the partners in a law firm, having participated in a writing and editing workshop with an outside consultant, might organize for their associates a mini workshop on several of the topics covered.

Third, are people inside and outside the organization commenting favorably—for example, about shorter, more concise and more comprehensible reports, briefs and correspondence?

Fourth, are a few of the participants submitting articles to journals or marketing copy to department heads?

And fifth, are the organization's proposals generating more support and funding than before the workshop was given?

A written evaluation completed by participants immediately after the workshop is one indicator of success, but the five questions listed above are a more significant measure of results.

Wise Words: Specific comments from participants, coupled with specific results, help gauge a workshop's effectiveness.

Selecting the
Right Consultant

Selecting an appropriate consultant is not easy. When selecting a skills trainer, first make sure that the person is not only a practitioner but a master of the skill he or she is going to teach. To teach people who are experts in their fields, one must be an expert in his or hers.

For example, few if any company employees faced with a major lawsuit would hire a lawyer who has taught litigation but has never tried a case. Nor would a company hire, to balance its books, an accountant who had never done an audit. A public speaking consultant should be a professional public speaker. Likewise, a writing consultant should be a well-published writer and an outstanding editor with experience in teaching adults. He or she also should have an excellent background in English.

Second, the trainer should have worked with many groups similar to the group he or she is about to encounter. A successful junior high school teacher may not be able to adapt to a room full of 35-year-old bank managers.

And finally, the training must focus on the specific problems of the group to be trained. One of the best training sessions I ever attended, on negotiation skills, was given by two dynamic and experienced Baltimore lawyers. The participants were directly involved in the entire session, making it not only beneficial but also enjoyable.

Every time an employee goes away to be trained and takes time from his or her job, the company loses money. Therefore, the training an employee receives should be so outstanding that the employee becomes twice as productive and is able to share newfound skills with co-workers and subordinates. You've probably heard the old maxim: "Those who can, do; those who can't, teach." When it comes to training, look for experts who both *do* and *teach*.

A CHECKLIST FOR CHOOSING
AN OUTSIDE CONSULTANT

1. *Educational background.* Does the consultant have appropriate undergraduate and graduate degrees?

2. *Relevant experience.* Does the consultant practice what he or she teaches?

3. *Similar groups.* Is the consultant experienced in dealing with large law firms, high-tech start-ups, mid-size accounting firms, architectural and engineering firms, and so on?

4. *Method.* Will the consultant use only partici-pants' work? *How will this be done?*

5. *Sharing.* Will the workshop be interactive? Will participants be able to learn from and help each other, as well as others in the company, after the course is over? Or will the participants be isolated and totally dependent on the instructor?

6. *Supervision.* Who supervises the consultant? Is he or she alone, or part of a group gaining feedback and insight from other professionals?

7. *Evaluation.* How will the course be evaluated? Will the training director, department head, or continu-ing education partner receive copies of the evaluations immediately after the workshop is completed?

8. *Number of participants.* If there are more than 10, individual attention and meaningful interaction are al-most impossible.

9. *Interest.* Does the workshop sound enjoyable?

Wise Words: Would *you* want to take the course or workshop?

NOTES:

NOTES:

NOTES:

NOTES:

NOTES:

NOTES: